Mar'24
Mar'23 4/1/10
Jun'22 4/0/1

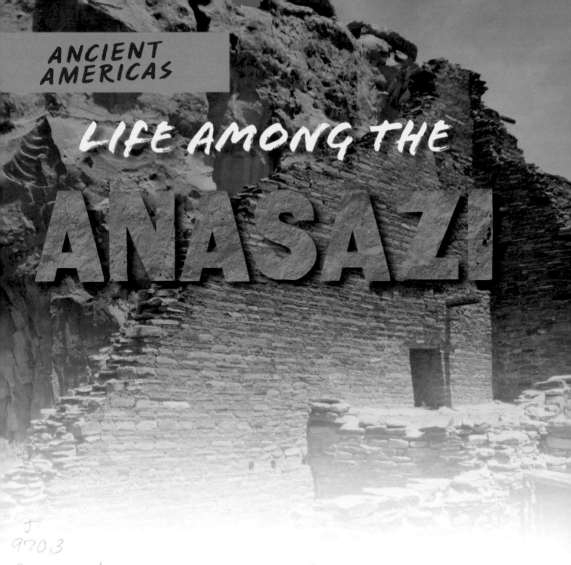

ANCIENT
AMERICAS

LIFE AMONG THE

ANASAZI

RACHEL STUCKEY

PowerKiDS
press™

NEW YORK

Published in 2017 by **The Rosen Publishing Group, Inc.**
29 East 21st Street, New York, NY 10010

Developed and produced for Rosen by BlueAppleWorks Inc.

Art Director: Haley Harasymiw
Managing Editor for BlueAppleWorks: Melissa McClellan
Editor: Marcia Abramson
Design: T.J. Choleva

Picture credits: Cover: bkgrd. pedrosala/Shutterstock; frgrd. cpaulfell/Shutterstock. Back cover: bkgrd.
altanaka/Shutterstock; frgrd. Artishok/Shutterstock. Title page: Rationalobserver/Creative Commons; p. 5
Steve Bower/Shutterstock; p. 9 KAZMAT/Shutterstock; p.10 inset, 13 Zack Frank/Shutterstock; p. 10 photogal/
Shutterstock; p. 12 inset kravka/Shutterstock; p. 12 Steven C. Price/Creative Commons; p. 13 inset left, 13
inset right Andreas F. Borchert/Creative Commons; p. 15 sumikophoto/Shutterstock; p. 15 inset Mavrick/
Shutterstock; p. 17 left Daderot/Public Domain; p. 17 middle Brooklyn Museum/Public Domain; p. 17 right
National Park Service /Public Domain; p. 17 marekuliasz/Shutterstock; p. 18 ir717/Shutterstock; p. 18 inset
Yourcelf/Creative Commons; p. 21 Ken Lund/Creative Commons; p. 22 inset NASA/Public Domain; p. 22 Bob
Adams/Creative Commons; p. 24 Henry F. Farny /Public Domain; p. 25 Public Domain; p. 27 Thomas Moran/
Public Domain; p. 29 Gimas/Shutterstock; Maps: T.J. Choleva/Bardocz Peter/Shutterstock; p. 9 inset T.J.
Choleva/AridOcean/Shutterstock

Cataloging-in-Publication Data
Names: Stuckey, Rachel.
Title: Life among the Anasazi / Rachel Stuckey.
Description: New York : PowerKids Press, 2017. | Series: Ancient Americas | Includes index.
Identifiers: ISBN 9781508149842 (pbk.) | ISBN 9781508149781 (library bound) | ISBN 9781508149668 (6 pack)
Subjects: LCSH: Pueblo Indians--Juvenile literature. | Pueblo Indians--Antiquities--Juvenile literature. |
Southwest, New--Antiquities--Juvenile literature.
Classification: LCC E99.P9 S78 2017| DDC 979'.01--dc23

Manufactured in the United States of America
CPSIA Compliance Information: Batch #BS16PK: For Further Information contact Rosen Publishing, New York, New York at 1-800-237-9932

CONTENTS

CHAPTER 1

ANCIENT ANASAZI

The Anasazi people lived for over a thousand years in the Four Corners region of the United States, where Utah, Arizona, New Mexico, and Colorado meet. Today's Pueblo peoples, including the Hopi, Zuni, Acoma, and Laguna, are the descendants of the Anasazi. The Anasazi are also known as the Ancestral Puebloans. The name Pueblo comes from the Spanish word for "village." In the 1500s, Spanish explorers used the name to describe the **adobe** and stone buildings in the Southwest where the Pueblo people lived. By that time, the Anasazi had long abandoned their own unique stone dwellings called great houses, which were built along canyon floors, on top of steep **mesas**, and along cliff walls in the Four Corners. There are no historical records of the Anasazi culture. Instead, we've learned about them through **archaeology.** Today the various Pueblo peoples of the Southwest share many cultural characteristics with their ancestors. That is how we know they are Anasazi descendants. Sometime around A.D. 1300, the original Anasazi cultures abandoned their great settlements and disappeared.

There is no single tribe or ethnic group called the Anasazi. Instead, archaeologists use artifacts and architecture to identify the culture.

ANCIENT PUEBLOANS BUILT DWELLINGS BENEATH THE CLIFFS IN THE MESA VERDE AREA IN COLORADO, STARTING ABOUT 1190. BEFORE THAT THEY LIVED ON TOP OF THE MESAS.

Throughout the region of the Four Corners, the buildings and objects discovered by archaeologists share similar characteristics. These characteristics show that the people who made them shared a similar culture. The **oral history** of modern Pueblo peoples also tells us about their ancestors. The Anasazi had a unique style of baskets, pottery, tools, and of course their famous buildings and settlements. Archaeological evidence shows that the great Anasazi civilization reached its height between A.D. 800 and 1300, a few hundred years before any Europeans arrived in the Southwest. But archaeologists are still debating when this culture first emerged. Some archaeologists believe the Anasazi developed from the Oshara, an **archaic culture** that lived in the region from around 5000 B.C. to around A.D. 400.

☐ Four Corners states
● Four Corners region

WHAT'S IN THE NAME?

No Native American group ever called itself the Anasazi. About 70 years ago, historians picked up the name from Navajo workers who were helping at archaeological sites in the Four Corners. The name Anasazi means "ancient enemy" or even "alien" in Navajo. The workers used that name because the ancient people who had lived in the sites were unknown to them.

Today many native groups prefer to use the name Ancestral Puebloans, which does not make anyone sound like an enemy. One group, the Hopi, use a different word, Hisatsinom, which means "ancient people" in their language. Other groups, though, do not want to give preference to a Hopi name.

PEAK AND DECLINE

Between A.D. 500 and 900, the number of Anasazi settlements increased and the population grew. Researchers know this period was good for agriculture by studying tree rings, which shows the amount of snow and rain. The Anasazi culture began to peak around this time. For example, researchers believe the population of southwestern Colorado was over 20,000—which is similar to the population in the region today. The most impressive examples of Anasazi architecture come from the period of A.D. 1000 to 1200. But in the late 1200s, the Anasazi began to abandon their great houses and settlements. By A.D. 1300, the population seems to have disappeared from the Four Corners. The ancestors of today's Navajo people moved into the Four Corners around A.D. 1400. But modern Puebloan people tell us that their ancestors did not just disappear—they simply moved into new territories.

CHAPTER 2

ANASAZI HOMELAND

The Four Corners region of the Southwest is part of the Colorado Plateau. A plateau is a large, flat high ground. The Colorado Plateau ranges from 4,500 to 8,500 feet (1,372 to 2,591 m) in elevation. Throughout the plateau there are large mesas, which are steep rock formations that are flat on top. There are many types of rock on the plateau, including limestone, sandstone, and shale. Wind and water **erosion** has created canyons and sandstone formations. The sandstone formations often look like someone has carved windows and bridges in the canyons. There are also limestone and sandstone overhangs which are created when the shale below is eroded more quickly. The Anasazi often built their stone dwellings beneath these overhangs for shelter and protection.

The region is mostly desert. There are also pine forests of juniper, pinyon, or ponderosa pines. Each type of tree grows better at a different elevation. But the area was very dry and there were often **droughts**. Summer rain was unpredictable and there were often thunderstorms. The Anasazi relied on the snow from the high elevations for water. The **porous** layers of sandstone collected snow melt and created springs and **seeps**.

SPIDER ROCK IS ONE OF THE FAMOUS FORMATIONS ON THE VAST COLORADO PLATEAU. THE NAME "COLORADO" IS SPANISH FOR "COLORED." SOME OF THE ROCKS THERE ARE MORE THAN A BILLION YEARS OLD.

Colorado Plateau region

9

MANY TOURISTS VISIT CLIFF PALACE AT MESA VERDE IN COLORADO. THE WHITE HOUSE RUINS (INSET) ARE IN THE NAVAJO NATION IN ARIZONA, WITH PEOPLE LIVING NEARBY.

BUILDINGS AND SETTLEMENTS

At the height of their civilization, the Anasazi had a large network of towns and settlements. By A.D. 900, the Anasazi started using complicated **masonry** and built walls with shaped stones that they quarried and transported far distances. Their many different buildings had multiple levels and rooms. Some rooms were even big enough to hold over a hundred people. The multi-room buildings and villages looked like modern apartment buildings. Some settlements were built into cliff walls, and others were built on the top of steep mesas. These were very good defensive positions to help protect against intruders. The complexes built by the Anasazi of Chaco Canyon were the largest buildings in North America until the 1800s.

KIVAS AND GREAT HOUSES

The large stone complexes of the Anasazi are known as great houses or pueblos. Archaeologists believe the various rooms of the great houses served different purposes. Some were for living in, others for food storage, and some for religious ceremonies.

The Anasazi also built kivas, which are rooms that are dug into the ground. Modern Pueblo peoples use kivas for religious rituals. But the early Anasazi used them for storage and residences as well. Many Anasazi settlements include great kivas. Great kivas are different from other kivas because they are larger and separate from the residence buildings. They also have walls that rise above the ground. They included benches around the edges of the room. Archaeologists believe great kivas were used for public ceremonies and religious purposes. Smaller kivas are subterranean rooms entered with a ladder. Kivas were probably sacred chambers for smaller religious ceremonies. Today's kivas play an important role in Puebloan religious tradition.

Cities in the sky

The Anasazi often built settlements atop tall mesas to help them stay safe. They used ropes or ladders to help them get up to their cities in the sky. If an animal or enemy threatened, they pulled up the rope or ladder.

11

ANASAZI ROADS

In Chaco Canyon, one of the major sites of Anasazi culture, there is a system of roads connecting the different settlements and sites outside the canyon. The largest roads were built around the same time as the great house sites, between A.D. 1000 and 1125. The roads were first discovered by archaeologists at the end of the nineteenth century, but **excavation** and study only began in the 1970s.

Using satellite images and excavations, archaeologists have identified over 180 miles (290 km) of roads. These roads are not just simple walking trails or paths—many of the roads are 30 feet (9 m) wide, which is the width of a modern two-lane highway.

The Anasazi also carved large ramps and stairways into the cliffs, which connect the roads at the top of the

THE ANASAZI CARVED STEPS TO GO UP CLIFFS. THESE WERE OFTEN STEEP AND THEY LIKELY USED ROPES TO HELP THEM.

WOOD WAS BROUGHT IN FROM FORESTS MILES AWAY TO HELP BUILD ANASAZI PUEBLOS SUCH AS THIS FAMOUS ONE IN CHACO CANYON IN NEW MEXICO.

canyons to their settlements in valleys below. Some of the roads also lead from the settlements to springs, lakes, and the tops of mountains.

Archaeologists disagree on the purpose of these roads. Some believe the purpose was religious and the roads were part of ceremonies. But others believe the real purpose was **economic**. At some sites archaeologists have found **luxury** goods such as **exotic** birds, marine shells, and turquoise. These goods would have been brought from other locations, and were probably traded along the road system. The roads could also have been used for transporting construction materials such as timber from faraway mountains. Some researchers have suggested the purpose of the roads was to quickly move a large army, which is why the Romans built roads. But there is no archaeological evidence that a large army existed.

13

CHAPTER 3

LIFE IN ANASAZI CIVILIZATION

The multi-room pueblos of the Anasazi ranged from 20 to 1,000 rooms. But each story or level of a pueblo was built back from the level below, which created terraces. Most of everyday life happened outside on the rooftops or terraces. The indoor spaces were used for sleeping and working in bad weather.

While the Anasazi were farmers, they also hunted and gathered wild plants. Many of the rooms in a pueblo were for food storage and preparation. They dried corn and squash, and stored nuts and sunflower seeds. Women likely spent hours every day grinding corn into flour. They also dried meat for storage—both large animals like bighorn sheep and small animals like mice and rabbits.

SOCIAL STRUCTURE

Researchers do not know very much about the social structure of Anasazi life. Modern Pueblo peoples are matriarchal—that means that land is owned by women, and children inherit land from their mothers. Clan affiliation also comes from the mother, and a husband traditionally joins his wife's family. This is the opposite of most Western culture. However, men usually hold the jobs of chief and religious leaders in modern Puebloan communities.

ARCHAEOLOGISTS NOW BELIEVE THAT
CLIFF PALACE HAD 150 ROOMS AND
23 KIVAS FOR A POPULATION OF ABOUT 100.

15

It's likely that these traditions came from the social practices of the Anasazi. The archaeological record cannot give us this information, but the oral traditions of the Puebloan peoples tell us that their ancestors were matriarchal.

The historical record suggests that there was a great deal of equality among the Anasazi. They probably all worked together to build their settlements. Later in their history they likely developed into clans with leaders. Archaeologists believe these leaders did have higher status, based on their burial sites.

FARMING METHODS

The Anasazi were farmers. They began as hunters and gatherers, but eventually learned to grow their own food through dry farming. In dry farming, farmers rely on the moisture in the soil that comes from snow melt, summer rains, and springs instead of using irrigation from a river. Dry farming was only possible at an elevation of about 6,800 feet (2,070 m). The temperatures were too cold at higher elevations and the lower elevations were too dry.

Turkeys

Turkeys were domesticated by early native people. At first the Anasazi kept them as pets and for feathers, which were used in rituals and clothing. By A.D. 1100, they knew that turkeys were good for dinner, too!

The people would care for the plants through spring and summer, growing corn, beans, and squash. Archaeologists believe the Anasazi were able to produce a large amount of food on a small amount of land by carefully tending the crops, which means they practiced intensive farming. This helped support a very large population of people throughout the region.

ARTS AND CULTURE

Ancient cultures usually begin making pottery once they begin farming because pottery is better than baskets for storing food. Anasazi food storage and cooking pots were gray and unpainted. A more ceremonial or formal type of pottery had black designs painted on white or light gray backgrounds.

ANASAZI POTTERY WAS DECORATED WITH GEOMETRIC DESIGNS OR DEPICTIONS OF PEOPLE, TREES, OR ANIMALS. THE DESIGNS HELP ARCHAEOLOGISTS IDENTIFY DIFFERENT GROUPS.

This style is still used by modern Pueblo pottery makers. Anasazi pottery is known for bold geometric patterns in black-on-white backgrounds, with some animal and human figures.

The Anasazi also created **petroglyphs** in the sandstone cliffs, often with similar geometric designs. Archaeologists do not know what the designs mean. The spirals may represent the movement of the sun or the passage of time. In some places, the sun hits different spirals at different times of the year, which means the petroglyphs may be a calendar. Modern Pueblos say that some of the symbols reflect clan membership. Other symbols, such as animal figures, may have been part of religious rituals.

NATIVE PEOPLES INCLUDING THE ANASAZI RECORDED STORIES IN PETROGLYPHS THAT CAN BE SEEN TODAY AT SITES INCLUDING NEWSPAPER ROCK AND HORSESHOE CANYON (INSET) IN UTAH.

EXPERT SKY WATCHERS

The Anasazi based their culture on nature, including the movement of the sun, moon, and stars. Anthropologists believe they studied the sky carefully and passed down their impressive knowledge of astronomy through the generations. This helped them know when to plant and harvest their crops, and when important astronomical events such as the **solstice** and the **equinox** should be celebrated.

Archaeologists think that the Anasazi laid out the buildings and roads at settlements such as Chaco Canyon in New Mexico and Chimney Rock in Colorado to line up with their astronomical observations. A petroglyph at Chaco Canyon, now called the Sun Dagger, appears to track the movement of the sun, while structures at Chimney Rock show that the Anasazi understood the lunar cycle as well.

RELIGION AND WORSHIP

Archaeologists have some theories about the beliefs and rituals of the Anasazi. They combine archaeological findings with the modern Puebloan beliefs and their oral traditions. In modern Puebloan traditions, kachinas are ancestral spirit beings who bring rain. Part of the kachina cult included worshiping the sun, fire, and snakes for **fertility** and good harvest.

As farmers, the Anasazi needed to watch the seasons and observe the lunar cycles. This is how they knew when to plant and harvest their crops. They probably had rituals to celebrate the winter and summer solstice and the harvest season.

CHAPTER 4

THE GOLDEN AGE

As the population grew, the Anasazi began what researchers call the Golden Age. From 900 to around 1150, the climate was warm and rainfall was good. As the people developed their building and farming techniques the population increased. Many people moved into small outlier communities and trade was very common. But sometime in the mid-1100s, the people left the outlying communities and moved back into the large settlements with the apartment-building-sized pueblos. This period is called the Great Migration. It is around this time that the Anasazi built the large cliff dwellings with multiple levels and terraces. This is also when the population stopped growing. And by 1300, the Anasazi seem to just disappear.

Lost words

The Anasazi left no written language, and no one knows how they spoke. Experts believe they may have had more than one language because their culture was spread out over such a wide area. Modern Puebloans speak six different languages.

THE RUINS OF ANASAZI PUEBLOS TELL MUCH ABOUT THEM WHILE ALSO SHOWING THAT THEIR CULTURE VANISHED.

21

The great Anasazi houses and cliff dwellings in the Four Corners were all abandoned by A.D. 1300, 100 years before the Navajo migrated there and 250 years before the Spanish arrived.

Archaeologists work hard trying to come up with answers to the mystery of Anasazi disappearance. They have learned a lot about the Anasazi from their architecture. Archaeologists also have learned about the Anasazi from the art they left on the walls and the way they buried their dead. But the most useful source of information comes from their garbage piles, which archaeologists call middens. The middens hold information about the plants and animals the Anasazi ate, the tools they used, and the pottery they made.

MIDDENS HAVE BEEN FOUND AT PUEBLO BONITO IN CHACO CANYON, ONE OF THE LARGEST ANASAZI RUINS. THE INSET SHOWS HOW THE COMPOUND MIGHT HAVE LOOKED.

THE GREAT DROUGHT

Every civilization needs water, but the Anasazi faced at least two periods of drought as the climate warmed in the northern hemisphere between A.D. 900 and 1300. During the first drought, from 1130 to 1180, they managed by building dams, reservoirs, and irrigation systems. This likely encouraged more people to move into larger settlements where the water was stored. These adaptations were not enough, however, when an even worse period of drought struck from 1279 to 1299. The population had grown so much that the Anasazi could barely produce enough crops to feed them all even when there was enough water, so the Great Drought was devastating.

WHAT HAPPENED?

Archaeological evidence tells us that throughout their history, the Anasazi communities moved to new locations when environmental conditions changed. By the end of the Golden Age, the large communities such as Chaco Canyon probably had damaged their environment by using up the water sources, chopping down all the trees, and stripping the soil of nutrients by overplanting. The entire region also suffered from a 50-year drought that began in A.D. 1130.

As the drought limited the food supply, villages may have started to fight other villages over resources. They may have even raided other communities for supplies. At the end of the Golden Age, some communities moved away in search of better farmland and water sources.

MAKING POTTERY IS ONE OF THE TRADITIONS THAT LINK THE ANASAZI TO TODAY'S PUEBLOAN PEOPLES.

This may also be because they needed a location that was easier to defend, like the top of a mesa or along a cliff wall.

This internal conflict and the lack of resources made the Anasazi **vulnerable** to outsiders moving into their territory. Researchers believe nomadic tribes from California, such as the Utes, Shoshones, and Paiute peoples, moved onto the Colorado Plateau at this time. There is even archaeological evidence of violence at the end of the Anasazi period. Archaeologists have found collections of bodies that were not properly buried. In Dolores, Colorado, they found **dismembered** bodies and even signs of **cannibalism**. The Anasazi who survived all these challenges left the region forever by A.D. 1300.

WHERE DID THEY GO?

For centuries, it was believed that the mysterious Anasazi simply disappeared. Many popular books and TV shows say that the Anasazi "vanished." But we now know that the modern Pueblo peoples are descendants of the mysterious "ancient ones." The oral tradition of the Puebloan people tells us that their ancestors did not disappear. As the Anasazi population declined, and life on the Colorado Plateau got too difficult, the ancient ones simply migrated to new locations looking for better conditions. They mixed with other cultures in the west, south, and east. Archaeologists have discovered the influence of the Anasazi in other parts of the Southwest.

THE ANASAZI BUILT LOOMS AND WOVE CLOTH FROM MANY NATURAL MATERIALS, ESPECIALLY AFTER THEY BEGAN GROWING COTTON. THIS TRADITION OF WEAVING CONTINUES TODAY.

25

CHAPTER 5

HISTORY AFTER THE ANASAZI

Navajo herders moved into the Chaco Canyon a few hundred years after the Anasazi abandoned it. Their own ancestors had probably traded with the Anasazi. But the Navajo did not know what happened to the people who built the great stone dwellings. Today, the Navajo Nation occupies land just west of the canyon.

The first Spanish explorers or **conquistadors** traveled through the Southwest in the 1530s searching for gold. For the next few centuries, the Spanish empire controlled the territory and built settlements, such as modern-day Santa Fe. The Spanish referred to the adobe and stone dwellings built by the descendants of the Anasazi as pueblos, the Spanish word for "villages." Soon, all the native peoples who lived in similar dwellings were called Pueblos or Pueblo Indians.

Soon after the formation of the United States of America in 1776, explorers and settlers from the new country moved west. It wasn't long before the United States and the Spanish Empire fought a war over the territory. In 1848, the land of the Anasazi became a U.S. territory.

PUEBLO TRADITIONS, WITH THEIR LONG HISTORY, CONTINUED FIRST UNDER SPANISH AND THEN U.S. RULE.

27

DESCENDANTS

The modern Pueblo peoples include the Hopi, Keres, Towa, Zuni, and Tanoan. These cultural groups were known as Pueblos because of the stone and adobe apartment-style dwellings they lived in when the Spanish explorers arrived. These groups speak different languages and have some cultural differences, but they also share many traditions. Today's Pueblo peoples are descended from the Hohokam, the Mogollon, and the Anasazi.

The Navajo Nation also shares some ancestors with modern Pueblo peoples. When the Spanish settled in the Southwest, they enslaved the Pueblo peoples. In 1680, the Pueblo peoples led a revolt against the Spanish near Santa Fe. The Navajo and Apache joined the revolt, and the native groups forced the Spanish to abandon their settlement. But in 1693, the Spanish returned to take the territory and many of the Pueblo peoples escaped to live among the Navajo. The two cultures made marriages and shared cultural traditions. Many elements of modern Navajo culture come from the Pueblo peoples.

A place in time

Though they may be called "ancient ones," Anasazi culture developed much later than ancient Greece and other civilizations traditionally called "ancient." When the Anasazi were having their Golden Age, Europe was still in the Middle Ages.

ANASAZI LEGACY

There are many ongoing excavations of Anasazi sites as archaeologists continue to study the culture. The best way to see the legacy of the Anasazi is by visiting national parks in the United States. Mesa Verde National Park in Colorado, Chaco Canyon National Historical Park in New Mexico, and Hovenweep National Monument in Colorado and Utah have some of the best preserved Anasazi villages and settlements.

Today there are about twenty modern Pueblo communities in the Southwest. Many Pueblo peoples still live in and around their historical pueblo structures. These pueblos are the oldest inhabited communities in the United States. The pueblos do not have electricity or running water. Many residents live in modern homes on the reservation land surrounding the pueblos.

PEOPLE HAVE LIVED IN THE TAOS PUEBLO IN NEW MEXICO FOR A THOUSAND YEARS.

GLOSSARY

adobe: a type of clay that can be dried into bricks in the sun

archaeology: the study of human history through artifacts and excavating ruins

archaic culture: a culture from an earlier archaeological period in the Americas, usually before the first century A.D.

cannibalism: when a species, such as humans, eat the flesh of their own species

conquistador: the Spanish word for conqueror, applied to the early Spanish explorers who were part of the military

dismember: to cut off the limbs of a person or animal

drought: a period with little to no rainfall or snow in which the land dries up and agriculture fails

economic: having to do with money, trading, or wealth

equinox: when the sun crosses the equator and day and night are exactly the same length

erosion: when something gradually wears away, usually from wind and water

excavation: the digging out of the earth to reveal something below

exotic: the quality of being from a foreign land or faraway place

fertility: the ability to conceive children

luxury: something that is not necessary but brings status or comfort

masonry: building things out of stone

mesa: a steep hill with a flat top

oral history: the historical record that is passed from one generation to the next through story telling

petroglyph: a rock carving, usually on cave walls or large stone formations

porous: having very small holes that allow liquid to pass through

seep: a place where water oozes out of the ground slowly

solstice: when the sun reaches its highest point on the longest day of the year, or its lowest point on the shortest day of the year

vulnerable: being in danger of a physical or emotional attack

FOR MORE INFORMATION

BOOKS

Chamanara, Sohrab. *Ancient Pueblo Peoples "Anasazi."* Bloomington, IN: Xlibris, 2010.

Fay, Gail. *Secrets of Mesa Verde: Cliff Dwellings of the Pueblo.* North Mankato, MN: Capstone Press, 2014.

Warrior, Robert. *The World of Indigenous North America.* New York: Routledge, 2014.

WEBSITES

Due to the changing nature of Internet links, PowerKids Press has developed an online list of websites related to the subject of this book. This site is updated regularly. Please use this link to access the list:

www.powerkidslinks.com/aa/anasazi

INDEX